HOW TO QUIT YOUR JOB AND BECOME AN ENTREPRENEUR

A practical guide to quitting your job and becoming an entrepreneur

www.albertopoku.com/books

Albert Opoku

Copyright © 2023

All rights to this book are reserved. No permission is given for any part of this book to be reproduced, transmitted in any form or means; electronic or mechanical, stored in a retrieval system, photocopied, recorded, scanned, or otherwise. Any of these actions require the proper written permission of the author.

Published by

Printed in Ghana

Cover Design by:

Muzeyi Yelyen

PDF copy available at www.albertopoku.com/books

First Printing Edition, 2023

DDC 338.04 - - *dc* 21

ISBN: 978-9988-3-6230-0

Dedication

To the spirited entrepreneurs of Kumasi Entrepreneurship Community, Kumasi Konnet, Kumasi Tech Community, GhanaThink Foundation, Kumasi Arts Community, and the hapaSpace community—your collective passion and camaraderie have transformed challenges into stepping stones of growth.

You have been my biggest support network throughout my entrepreneurial journey. You have cheered me on when I was down, offered me advice when I needed it, and helped me to connect with other entrepreneurs. I am so grateful for your support and encouragement.

To all of you who have failed so many times but never gave up, you are a special breed. You have the courage to take risks, the determination to keep going, and the vision to see your dreams come true. I am inspired by your stories and I know that you will continue to achieve great things.

Albert Yaw Opoku

2023

Table of Contents

Introduction vi

Chapter One: In the veins 10

Chapter Two: The necessary boring stuff 14

Chapter Three: The business school called "work" 17

Chapter Four: Build capital 21

Chapter Five: Build a support network 25

Chapter Six: Quitting your job 29

Chapter Seven: No regrets 32

My other book: What I learnt Late - 52 Life Lessons 34

INTRODUCTION

I have been an entrepreneur for thirteen years, co-founding Hapaweb Solutions (www.hapaweb.com) and hapaSpace (www.hapaspace.com) in 2010 and 2023 respectively. Over these years, I have crossed paths with countless aspiring entrepreneurs, each with a gleam of possibility in their eyes and a longing to break free from the confines of their current jobs. Many have sought my guidance, asking the burning question, "**How do I quit my job and become an entrepreneur?**" This book, my dear reader, holds my answers.

I, too, once stood where you now stand—a dedicated employee with dreams reaching beyond the horizons of my workplace. In 2012, after months of reflecting on what I to do with my life, I took that daring leap and resigned from my job, a decision which has forever changed my life trajectory. Now, my mission is to light your path and guide you through the doubts, uncertainties, and exhilarating triumphs that lie ahead.

In these pages, I invite you to join me on a voyage of self-discovery and empowerment. I share the practical steps I took to traverse the metamorphic bridge from employee to employer, the very bridge that beckons you as well.

Throughout our journey together, you'll explore the depths of your passions and embrace the exciting dance between risk and reward. As we sail through the chapters, you'll gain the insights, wisdom, and courage to determine if this path is for you and, if so, how to conquer it.

Becoming an entrepreneur is not merely a career shift. It's a mindset, a lifestyle, and a chance to sculpt your destiny according to your dreams. The possibilities are as vast as the cosmos, waiting for you to reach out and seize them.

So, whether you're sipping tea at your desk, gazing at the horizon of change, or just curious about the world of entrepreneurship, this book offers a compass to navigate your aspirations. By the time you turn the final page, you'll be equipped with clarity, confidence, and a roadmap to your future—one you'll shape with your own hands.

I encourage you to share your thoughts and opinions with me through my email, 52@albertopoku.com. Now, let us set sail upon the sea of possibilities. Your journey as an entrepreneur awaits, and I am honoured to be your guide.

Bon voyage!

Albert Yaw Opoku

Entrepreneur and Co-founder

www.albertopoku.com/books

HOW TO QUIT YOUR JOB AND BECOME AN ENTREPRENEUR

A practical guide to quitting your job and becoming an entrepreneur

Onward to a world of endless potential

CHAPTER ONE: IN THE VEINS

I was raised in Kumasi, the second capital of Ghana and home to the biggest open market in West Africa. Growing up, every child in my neighbourhood had at least one parent who was an entrepreneur. My father was an architect, but made most of his income from the two building materials shops that he owned. My mother was a professional teacher, but was also a garment trader.

From age ten, I worked at my father's shops daily after school and during vacations. Right from an early age, I knew I would run my own business one day. Owning and running a business was already in my veins. When I had to select a course to pursue in high school, I chose to study business. Likewise, I studied business administration at the University of Ghana for my undergraduate degree.

During my four years at the University, I started several side hustles. I sold diskettes, CD- and DVD-ROMs, T-shirts, leather sandals and eggs. In my second year, I developed an interest in computer programming, and in my third year, I bought my first second-hand computer with my savings from three years of side hustles. Once I had the computer, I branched into IT-related businesses, including CD dubbing and SPSS data analytics. Through these businesses, I earned more money than the monthly allowance my parents sent me.

It was not always smooth sailing. In my second year, I lost all my capital after my stock of T-Shirts was stolen, and I had to live on gari (a fine to coarse granular flour of varying texture made from cassava tubers) for weeks until my student loan arrived. In my third year, a friend and I invested in retailing leather sandals. The business was booming until we enlisted a shoemaker on campus to sell the sandals on a profit-sharing agreement. He disappeared with all our stock, and I was back to living on gari for weeks until my next student loan arrived.

Despite all the losses and the need to start all over again, I was never in doubt about running my own business in the future. Although I did not realize it then, these side hustles at university helped me build resilience and a strong business acumen, which have served me well in my entrepreneurship journey.

Now, let's come to you. What's in your veins? You don't need to have come from a set of entrepreneur-parents, like I did, to have entrepreneurship in your veins. Nor, do you need to have grown up in a community where almost every adult has a business, like I did, to have entrepreneurship in your veins.

What you do need—and only you can really tell—is this: do you have what it takes to take risks? Do you have the discipline to save and build appreciable capital to invest in a venture? Can you handle losing everything and having to start all over again? If you do, then you may have entrepreneurship blood in your veins.

To help you discern whether entrepreneurship pulses within you, I've developed the "Entrepreneur's Self-assessment" questionnaire. Visit www.albertopoku.com/tools to gauge your entrepreneurial potential and discover if this path is meant for you.

Remember, self-employment or entrepreneurship is not for everyone! And that's perfectly fine. It's not a crime to prefer to be an employee. There are many satisfied and wealthy employees. If you recognise that entrepreneurship is not your cup of tea, do not let the ongoing hype about entrepreneurship make you feel unworthy or unaccomplished. Embrace your unique journey, whether it leads to entrepreneurship or a different path. That said, this book is for people who want to quit their jobs and become full-time entrepreneurs. If that resonates with you, that is good. This book is for you.

Let me reiterate. Having entrepreneurship in your veins is not about being born an entrepreneur. Yes, you may have been born with the qualities of an entrepreneur, but you could also assimilate these qualities as a result of your environment, or learnt them in school.

Whatever the case, you do need a burning desire to run a business, coupled with the fortitude to take risks and the mental and physical capacity to strive irrespective of multiple failures. Ultimately, the fire within you—the tenacity to endure and rise, time and again—will define your journey as an entrepreneur.

Onwards and upwards

CHAPTER TWO: THE NECESSARY BORING STUFF

In the vast landscape of entrepreneurship literature, countless books, courses, and articles explore the theoretical knowledge essential for aspiring entrepreneurs. However, this book has a distinct focus—it is not a conventional business training manual. Instead, our journey sidesteps the realms of traditional entrepreneurial teachings, delving into the practical steps required before making the transformative leap from employee to entrepreneur.

While I won't delve into the intricacies of ideation, business model canvases, business plans, or cash flow management, let me emphasise that this knowledge is crucial and should not be overlooked. I will highly recommend that you enter an incubation programme with any business hub or enterprise support organisation close to you. If you're based in Ghana, you can find a list of innovation and business hubs on the website of the Ghana Hubs Network: https://www.ghanahubsnetwork.com/.

Most of these hubs have incubation programmes that will enable you to learn the principles of validating a business idea, prototyping your product or service, developing a minimum viable product (MVP) and developing a go-to-market strategy. If you're outside Ghana but within Africa, check out the website of AfriLabs, the association of African hubs, for a hub in your country: https://afrilabs.com/.

Should your current employment situation impede your participation in a physical incubation programme, fret not. The digital realm offers an array of online entrepreneurship courses. You will find world-class courses for free on websites such as:

1. Alison - https://alison.com/tag/entrepreneurship
2. edX - https://www.edx.org/learn/entrepreneurship
3. Google Digital Garage - https://learndigital.withgoogle.com/digitalgarage
4. VC4A - https://academy.vc4a.com/entrepreneurship-course
5. MIT OpenCourseWare - https://ocw.mit.edu/collections/entrepreneurship

Know that engaging in these incubation programmes or pursuing online courses requires dedication, self-motivation, and considerable discipline. The journey may seem tedious or boring, but the knowledge you'll gain from these courses will serve you well when you finally take the plunge and start your own business.

These foundational steps might not be as glamorous as the vision of entrepreneurial success, but they form the bedrock upon which your venture shall rise. So, embrace the necessary groundwork with an open mind and a hunger for knowledge—it's a pivotal phase in shaping your entrepreneurial destiny.

Embrace your learning journey

CHAPTER THREE: THE BUSINESS SCHOOL CALLED "WORK"

Have you seen the tuition fees for a Master's in Business Administration (MBA)? An MBA course is usually one of the most expensive programmes offered by any university. The good news is, if you're currently an employee then you have the opportunity to earn an "MBA" not only for free, but you actually get paid while learning as well. If you view your place of work as a business school and not just a place for earning a wage, you'll realise that you have the opportunity to learn what it takes to make a business successful.

Any business that has grown beyond the founder(s) and has employed personnel—even if under five employees—has done some things right. As an employee, you have the unique opportunity to learn what it takes to make a business successful or not. Each day, you have the chance to grasp the intricacies of customer behaviour, product and service development, sales, finance, team performance, leadership, systems, processes, and much more. In a very large organisation, you may not work in all of these departments, but you would have colleagues in these departments and if you see your workplace as your "MBA" university, you can send time picking their brains to understand their roles and how to best curate these roles for a small business.

Although I learned a lot about entrepreneurship while working at my father's two building material shops, the five years I spent working at the British Council were the years that I learnt the importance of business systems, and how to create and automate workflow. I learnt how to manage and lead teams, understand HR policies and the importance of cash flow management. From project management to report writing, from stakeholder engagement to effective networking, every facet of business became a canvas for learning.

During my time at the British Council, I was always one of the first to volunteer for a training programme or attend an event that others would not attend. For me, I was bent on learning as much I as could from an organisation that had existed for over 75 years and operated in 110 countries. For me, being an employee at the British Council was not just about earning a wage, it was an opportunity to earn a world-class 'MBA' and get paid while doing so.

I entered the British Council as a young 25-year-old National Service personnel with a bachelor's degree in Business Administration. Within three years, I was the youngest office manager across all 110 countries where the British Council operated. Through online courses and YouTube videos, I ventured into IT and gained promotion as the Digital Service Manager for Sub-Saharan Africa, which meant I was responsible for the Council's web services across 13 countries.

If your sights are set on transforming from employee to entrepreneur, then you must have a similar mental attitude towards your current employment. Every day that you leave for work, you are leaving to attend an MBA class—a class where you learn and get paid for learning. Soak up all that you can learn from the organisation that you're working for. Don't do your work grudgingly. Don't join the people who always complain about one thing and another. If there's a problem, do your best to find a solution. Give your employer your very best. At the end of the day, this attitude will earn you a first-class degree during your "MBA studies" at the business school called "Work".

Empower yourself for the journey ahead

CHAPTER FOUR: BUILD CAPITAL

Let's recap. In chapter one, you identified whether you have entrepreneurship blood running in your veins. In chapter two, we covered how you can learn the boring stuff you need to know to succeed as an entrepreneur. Then in chapter three, we covered how at this moment that you're an employee, you're uniquely placed as an MBA student in the business school of "Work".

The first three chapters cover the foundations you have to put in place. In this chapter and the last one, we cover the next step—how to get started! You need two kinds of capital for your business: financial capital and human capital.

Let's consider financial capital. Whatever your business idea, you need funds to get it off the ground. You need funds to develop a Minimum Viable Product (MVP). An MVP is a version of your or service product with just enough features to be usable by early customers who can then provide feedback for future product development. And eventually, when you quit your job and no longer have a reliable monthly source of income, you'll need funds to cover your day-to-day living expenses.

As such, you need to build capital now. In my case, I did that in two ways. The last two years before I left the British Council and co-founded Hapaweb Solutions, I lived on half of my monthly salary and invested the other half in Treasury Bills. Was it easy to live on half of my salary? Of course, it wasn't! It was very tough. I had to forgo comforts and embrace frugality. It meant that I continued to eat gari and beans (gobe) at least three times a week, and although I was a Digital Service Manager, I could only afford to drive a small second-hand Opel Astra.

I was willing to make sacrifices because I needed to build capital. When I eventually left the British Council in 2010, I was able to survive the harsh realities of running a business, only because I had saved half of my salary for two years. It was these savings that kept me going during the difficult periods when the business was struggling to generate income.

The other means by which I raised capital was through a side hustle. I learnt website design on YouTube and www.w3schools.com. During the weekends, I was a freelance website developer. Sixty per cent of my earnings from website design was added to my Treasury Bills investment.

If you're going to quit your job to become an entrepreneur, embrace the art of postponed gratification. Manage your current finances in preparation for the turbulent period of getting your business off the ground. You would be surprised by how long it may take before your enterprise can start paying you a regular income. If you can, save half of your current earnings. And if you're murmuring that you don't earn enough to save some of it, then you have to look closely at your current financial commitments vis-à-vis your entrepreneurship ambitions.

Next, start a side hustle, and be very careful not to compete with your employer. You can offer services or products that are totally different or complementary to what your employer offers. Ethical conduct is paramount—never use your employer's time to work on your personal business. Respect the boundaries that uphold integrity. When your own business is up and running, you would not want your employees to steal your time for their personal businesses, so don't do the same.

If you are employed as an accountant, you can start a side hustle as an auditor for small businesses. If you are a chef, you could handle parties on your off days. Basically, extend your skills to others in a manner that does not conflict with your current job, but can earn you extra income.

Having covered financial capital, let's move on to human capital. You may have heard the saying "Your network determines your net worth". For your business, I'd like you to consider your network as a potential source of human capital. As an employee, you meet and interact with many people. You should use every interaction to grow your network—your human capital. Take and keep phone numbers and email addresses, and build relationships.

Chapter 41 of my book "What I Learnt Late – 52 Life Lessons" is titled *Stay in Touch with Your Network*. In this chapter, I've stated that it took me a while to figure out the importance of building and maintaining strong relationships, by constantly contacting the people I had met in various places. As a young professional, I knew the power of networks, so I consciously evolved from an introvert to an extrovert in order to build a strong network.

Building your human capital is not just about collecting and building a museum of business cards. It is not the phone number or the email address that is valuable; it is the human relationships that they enable you to build. Invest in building relationships while you are still an employee. A good number from your network have the potential of becoming your clients when you eventually quit your job and start your own business.

In unity and strength

CHAPTER FIVE: BUILD A SUPPORT NETWORK

At this point you're on course. You have set up the foundation for entering into the entrepreneurship phase of your life, and you're saving and building financial and human capital. This is also the time to find and build up a support network.

Entrepreneurship is hard. Very hard. It's an exhilarating but challenging path, filled with both triumphs and tribulations. There are great and exciting days, but there are also many low days - trust me, there will be plenty of days that you would want to give up and go back into the job market. You'll be frustrated; you'll work outrageous hours; your spirit will be brought low several times, and some days you'll cry. But you can handle it. It's all part of the exciting world of the entrepreneur.

To navigate the lows and savour the highs, you'll need a support network to ground, motivate, and encourage you during those low days. This is one of several reasons why having a co-founder is a good idea. You'll have someone who is going through this journey with you, someone who understands the frustrations and challenges, and someone you can celebrate and party with during the good days as well. A good co-founder can be the defining factor between success and failure in your entrepreneurial pursuit.

I have been fortunate to have two co-founders—Gideon and Ben. I met Gideon in high school. We were in the same class and house. After high school, we went to the same university, and there, worked together on several of the side hustles I mentioned in Chapter One. We both worked at the British Council, before founding Hapaweb Solutions. By the time we started Hapaweb, Gideon and I had been best friends for over fourteen years.

Gideon and I met Ben about a year after we started Hapaweb. We were going through hard times getting Hapaweb off the ground, and Ben, who was genuinely interested in Hapaweb, and is a few years older than Gideon and me, became like a supportive big brother. In fact, I can say, at some points, he had more belief in the success of Hapaweb than I did. He was a good fit for Gideon and me, so he joined us at Hapaweb, and we've been together since 2011. I can tell you with great certainty that Hapaweb would have long died if I had not had these two guys by my side.

Apart from having a co-founder(s) as part of your support network, you should find and engage with a community of entrepreneurs. Most of these communities hold networking events, training events, or conferences. Within these communities you'll find people who have traversed the path that you want to undertake. They'll understand your challenges and provide you with just the right word or encouragement when you need it, or a referral to a resource that will help you with a certain challenge.

I'm part of several of such communities, and I cannot emphasise enough how these communities can be a wellspring of wisdom and inspiration. Before I left the British Council, I was already a regular attendee of many GhanaThink Foundation events. GhanaThink Foundation, is a talent mobilization social enterprise, that runs programs in networking, mentoring, volunteering & training. I've always attended the GhanaThink Barcamp Ghana events and their Kumasi Konnect meetups, and through such events, I've met amazing people who are part of my great support system. I still attend many community events such as those by the Kumasi Entrepreneurs Community and meetups events at the various hubs in Kumasi.

All said and done, start building your support network of like-minded people—people in the entrepreneurship ecosystem—while you are still an employee. Your support network will be helpful at the point when you're quitting your job, when you get started and when you face the inevitable difficult times of running a business.

With foresight and fortitude

CHAPTER SIX: QUITTING YOUR JOB

In this chapter, we approach the pivotal moment of transitioning from employee to entrepreneur—a momentous decision that requires careful consideration and prudent planning. I intentionally used the word "Quitting" in the title of this chapter rather than the word "Quit", to indicate how this is an ongoing process. Based on my experiences and observations over the years, I would not advise that you quit your job and zoom straight into entrepreneurship. Take the proverbial baby steps. Give yourself a minimum "quitting" period of one year.

Before I left the British Council, I chose to transition from full-time to part-time employment. For a year, I divided my time, dedicating three days a week to the British Council and the remaining two days to Hapaweb Solutions. Looking back, if given a second opportunity, I would extend this part-time arrangement for at least another year before fully leaving my job.

Let me be very honest with you. Starting a business is hard and it's even harder in Africa. In Africa, you have to grapple with high cost of capital, regulatory barriers, poor infrastructure and limited access to markets. As someone accustomed to receiving a monthly salary, the uncertainty of an entrepreneur's income can be one of the most difficult realities to confront. This is another reason why you should have saved half your salary for at least two years prior to the start of your "quitting" phase.

If you can, start the business while you're still employed. It makes perfect sense to hire someone to run your business full-time for you while you are still employed. Your training, experience and skills developed over the years should help you put in place proper systems and structures that will enable you to supervise the activities of your business without your constant physical presence.

Let me say it one more time: don't rush to quit your day job! It's your current source of income and sustenance. Start the business, while still employed, even if it means that you have to start small or hire someone to handle the day-to-day operations.

Another reason why you should quit gradually is to allow your personal business to grow its capital base. Since you will not be drawing income from the business to meet your personal expenditure, you would be able to reinvest the majority of your profit back into the business and as such accelerate its growth. Otherwise, you will malnourish your fragile business if you quit your regular job and become dependent on it to cover your personal living expenses.

In my case, the two years of savings I accrued before leaving my job provided the cushion I needed. It meant I did not require any salary from my start-up in the first two years. But even with those savings, I struggled. It took five years, from 2010 to 2015, before Hapaweb Solutions was able to pay me half the salary I'd received at the British Council. Those three years between 2012 and 2015, when my savings ran out and Hapaweb was still struggling, were the most difficult and darkest moments of my life so far. That's why in hindsight, I would have spent more than a year as a part-time employee at the British Council, before leaving to start Hapaweb.

One last thing. Before you hand in that resignation letter, spend an hour writing up at least five reasons why you want to quit your job. The paper size should fit into your pocket or purse so that you can carry it around. Write your reasons for quitting on a cardboard or on a piece of paper that you can laminate so it's durable enough for you to carry around for years.

During the hard times of entrepreneurship, it's so easy to forget why you quit your job in the first place and decided to enter the turbulent world of entrepreneurship. You will need this card and its reasons to remind you why you left.

During the very low days, when sleep deserts you, when worries fill you up, when you have no money, and yet mounting bills to pay, the one thing you may remember so fondly about the job that you quit will be your monthly salary. You will question why the heck you gave that up for this difficult life. During those moments, you will need this card and its reasons to remind you why you left. Trust me, this card and its reasons will serve as a poignant reminder during moments of doubt or struggle.

CHAPTER SEVEN: NO REGRETS

As I reflect on my journey, from my years as an employee at the British Council, to my current role as an entrepreneur, I am filled with gratitude for the invaluable lessons and experiences that have shaped me. As I emphasised in Chapter Three, my five years at the British Council (2005 - 2010) were a great learning experience that equipped me with vital skills that have proven to be indispensable on my entrepreneurial path. Now, thirteen years since I left my job, I can confidently say that while entrepreneurship has been far from easy, it has been profoundly rewarding.

While the darkest and most difficult moments of my life have all occurred during my entrepreneurship journey, overall, I do not have any regrets about quitting my job thirteen years ago and becoming an entrepreneur.

For me, entrepreneurship was in my veins, but I want to emphasise that entrepreneurship is not a path for everyone. There's no shame if you don't have the same burning desire to be an entrepreneur. If the burning desire to be an entrepreneur is absent, it's perfectly fine to pursue other avenues. Entrepreneurship is not a prerequisite for success or fulfilment.

For those who possess the entrepreneurial spirit and are contemplating quitting their jobs, I leave you with these suggestions:

1. Be sure this is what you want: Thoroughly evaluate your aspirations and motivations. Ensure that entrepreneurship aligns with your vision and values.

2. Learn the boring stuff about business: Acquire the foundational knowledge necessary for entrepreneurship. Seek out incubation programmes, online courses, and resources to sharpen your business acumen.

3. Use your employment to gain an 'MBA' degree: Embrace your current job as a learning ground. Treat it like a business school where you can acquire invaluable skills that will benefit your entrepreneurial journey.

4. Build your financial and human capital: Save and invest diligently, preparing yourself for the challenges of entrepreneurship. Also, build meaningful relationships within the entrepreneurship ecosystem to form a strong support network.

5. It is quitting, not quit: Consider a gradual transition from employee to entrepreneur. Allow yourself a minimum of a year to ease into entrepreneurship while continuing part-time employment or hiring someone to manage your business.

As you embark on your own path, I wish you all the best in your entrepreneurial endeavours. The journey may be challenging, but with determination and perseverance, you will overcome obstacles and reach new heights.

I look forward to welcoming you to the other side of the fence. You can always share your thoughts and opinions with me through my email, 52@albertopoku.com.

MY OTHER BOOK: WHAT I LEARNT LATE - 52 LIFE LESSONS

If you have enjoyed reading this book, I encourage you read my other book titled: **What I learnt Late - 52 Life Lessons.** Get a copy from www.albertopoku.com/books

Reviews

"In this book, Albert shares from a place of compassion, openness, and sincerity. Especially in a generation where there is so much desire to present a perfect picture, Albert bares it all and presents the lessons he has learned in a simple, straightforward, and relatable manner. I look forward to the other books that will follow this one and fully and completely endorse this debut work as a must-read for everyone. "

Petra Aba Asamoah | Marketing Executive, Writer & Author

"Fantastic. I have always wondered how a book that Albert finally decides to write will look and feel like. I'm glad to say it is exactly as I thought. Witty, funny, straight to the point and still profound. This book manages to compress a lifetime of life lessons in very short chapters that can be read at a sitting. The bonus is you get to learn in a few hours what has taken him over four decades to know. Definitely recommended."

Dr. Samuel Tinagyei | Optometrist, Author and Certified Master Coach.

"What a delightful read!!! I haven't picked up a book and read it cover to cover in ages. I truly love the content, as I could practically identify with most, if not all, you said. Truly something to share with my boys and their generation as it addresses issues clearly that I would love to have shared with them if I could put it in to words. I do appreciate this. Thank you for sharing and overcoming your fear of writing. I am certain, that you will certainly exceed sales of over 10,000 copies, trust me!"

Philip Agbese Jnr. | Co-founder, CAVIC

"An incredibly succinct compass for any young person, with lots of nuggets of truth for the older reader. It should be a bedside reader, right next to where the scripture book is! From a first-time author, this is a well-written piece both engaging and inspiring...you almost want to yell 'aha' at the end of every page. The lessons are at the core of the human enterprise, love, money, getting things done and enjoying the journey, and having Albert's road map to help one along the way is especially wonderful."

Juliet A. Amoah | Country Director at Emerging Public Leaders

THE END

www.albertopoku.com/books

www.ingramcontent.com/pod-product-compliance
Lightning Source LLC
Chambersburg PA
CBHW031558210526
45464CB00003B/1332